BREACH

Lisa Samuels's *Breach* is a meditation on the material of contagion. In terrifyingly precise helicoid strands of words hinging and unhinging from the order of grammar, Samuels unravels in poetic nucleotides the warp and weft of our different transnational pathogens knotting into monuments at the breach of biopolitical capitalism, from the everyday of breath as windows, to the felt rend(er)ing of our data flows, our "crypt toes". The first work of poetry I have read that has helped me think-feel COVID, really, the way it is changing the relationship between inside and out, and the personal-political metaphysics of materialism, as body, as power, and as language. A vaccine against the solitude of screen heritage, confinement, and fear.
　—Lily Robert-Foley

Written in the pandemic that broke so many of us open, Lisa Samuels' *Breach* pieces together the body that the Spinoza epigraph suggests "constitutes the formal being of the human mind." Lines and words cohabit, fragment, and trail down the page, making new meanings and associations as this book considers relations among *mind*, *body*, and *human*, terms whose foundations have been unsettled by the pandemic, authoritarian brutality, and intense isolation of 2020-2021. In this polymorphous text pleasure and pain coexist, "ear to ear / composite / lustening," and each touch is haunted by the breach it must cross to meet another. If we listen with more than our ears perhaps we can peer "underneath / your skein face / doctor, nurse" and develop "ideas of what's / sheer." Sheered open, we might make ourselves a little more transparent, a little less masked.
　—Amaranth Borsuk

BREACH

LISA SAMUELS

BOILER HOUSE PRESS

Idea, quae esse formale humanae mentis constituit,
est idea corporis

The idea which constitutes the formal being of the
human mind is the idea of the body

   —Baruch Spinoza, *The Ethics*
   (English translation Samuel Shirley)

1

Naming the window
penny filter
stirs a sight oblique
the line
Li Wenliang
or next
garden toil
I awoke tilted after
communiqués
guards
the grocery aisles
aqualungs on speakers
who could tell
Li Wenliang any
thing?

Sheer window
treatment
passing thru
room to
savage room

treatise on nice
felt coasters
shaking
the ice cup
linear equilibrates
one coast line
hankering
for shore

ready to the lips
dictates wait
postures
waving at windows
water splish here
tankards writ
every which
day there too
dreamt
integument circles
those sweet green
carve caves
thru whom
treats of suffering are
over there
sit stead
worrit
for the plug fair
it'll be in
arrears the spots of

time turned in
to busy modes the
conversation occurs
amidst some other
Li Wenliang than
here the terriers
nab incessant quiet
perky jointers
paka pak paka pak
the trucks are
on the road and
in front of

factizing re places
one is and is not
bare there happy to
think of some
one absent
more than one
if 'everything's connected'
waves of silicate or
personage flicks
over in-
side others
and what's with
having drunk
advices? one's
only doing the bet
one can

a drink out of
domestibles
current spike in
contact

thereby we re-
cognize
the local's
far more self-
infused it's
not coral close to
sea size
necessaire but
'something in the water'
one drinks media
telly one
supers holding
out your
cup receipt
hold your mouth a
truth pours in
from outside
what

Every stand in time we
are to dance sing clinic
get the
die We are to stay
a place keep close
things go
out Listen to the
lead or not to
sort of ecohealth breath
diets flanged by
small experience
holding out the cup
keep company
keep some trail out
indices of leader
ship its mind
a floating out of formerly
probable local
dominance to a fatuous
globál

sort of starting there
Li Wenliang
with a mouth on
a bleeding
edge of
agribusiness in-
timates where
warmer maps have
pathogens in patterns

we could choose
or that's the
fict
this strips off
veils one might
collect or
cling with
paisley in the ripples
chips on
brain might
like the pats
on circumvention
we could sort of
suck the veil
its wet-on habit
stampede we in
mailings for the cult
you're sure
Li Wenliang
you have it
right?

A numb field
not for noth-
ing have we

kept the Pantry full
for you funded in-
patient
parts there the
limbs tumble
down slit
from the anatomy
of linens
slung for bet

you in the morning
checks falling out
the mail slot your
eye-fingers
dubious eternity
of luminous toast
jam pot of fire
disks funded by palm
soap strip air
brush steel age
pulled themselves from
remembering then
but it were
happen to whomed?
it were not
then Li Wenliang
but 'one death is a tragedy'
and many consume
all our def
statistics

you turn the door
knob to
discover
air

In the field
we're tether balling our
dreamy eyes
gone out for soup
some fun
derived the out-
breaks
back to
origin's tough sweet
we chew it
toughing-
ly the fact of
every answer being
the one you swill
today so then
the orient and
tongue of that
horizon's just
the resolution we
for death to
seeked

and once
you've got it
then the answer
owns for air

fly wing
near that
still soaked in
absolute geographies

the window
treats the wind
air finds airs
there's no cut
sound comes
any bird
throats the
earthy oxygen or
trees so far
we're always getting
'there'

our fatal-
ism tropes for
twist and
earnings
popular extractivist
so call credits
for the sweet
exterior
threats of
groceries
hands on techno
maps and wild-type
host societies
land pool-
ing generous
shifts in lumps
the bodies oh
well

transferrals
ghosts on walls
on dreams
where Li Wenliang
be
comes

The wash goes
periurban
diets licked
for core
necessitas
the heart's own
sweetmeats what do
they a company
from damage in a
trade you for
a coaster you can
leave it at the
top between
the building blocks
some body's piled
balance
sheets
their linen
current
having it for the air

in elemental
epidemes
one could at
tribute
newspapers or
finger swipes

the steles of our
washing up
drip
over every hint-
erland admission

pin a pathogen
fair city clip
the doorway
waves it can
articulate on
to where the rolling
rounder sap
fell where
taught breath
sucked in
words and
image flusters
colon ate it up or
backward realize
strips of normalcy
work
how don
our country close

the wiggle mat
we step on in
between the
air and window
curtain where
the glass
is made to breathe
but very
slowly
be
yond what
we can administer
our selves
an elocution
arm

someone who'll
sit and tether to
mobility
what continuous
education? what value
metals dripping off
this interstice
of skip from where
a starter tip
who isn't
Li Wenliang
any
more whose
space where
blood do sang

the wash hangs
organized
exacerbate
multi-febrile every
exponent since
months were
want to bring a
plan they
forage in the
fertile waste
starts pillage every
point

Home burials
made of money
food
now flexibly de-
coup
a cardboard
reason

ash silts a core
depile between
your city
definitions
fleshly once
again
you pet domestic
ambiance and
wash your pyre

they're sat there
with their
opiates and extraction
trade and wanters in-
divisible from
how the mouths
pop pop
connect

one dances on a rope
another twirls another
picks sylvatic

pathogens
in the pipes
you put
anything on top
of cut
containment
fields the question
nowhere's
not too far
the bed's a major
architecture co-
dependent lung

a scurry tuck
infolds
wet lips a
cram of sur-
reality zaps its
curtains all
too well turned
in electro-
cute cost out
your pocky mouth
ex or able to spill
splotch cup
in frame
by tiny thousands

oh I have to
Li Wenliang
although
one doesn't know
just anything
without
the moan of some
home engine work
school friends in
delicate
nothing's out of nature
parse of air

2

The hypertrophic bell
extends its in-
famy
well you can see
the culture sit-in
at the face? whose
magnets
purl the screen
or come refrigerate
in cluster alpha-
bets bit cut
another given
mealtime in
commodity country
outbreak model
dishing at the spoon
not run away

packed
foil dishes
in some stars

we're hungry all
the time re-
collecting what
shared breath
that donnish spirit-
ual kitsch
on a plate all about
presentation
movies taught us
everything
we know
how to falter accent-
ually how to
give big hugs to
distance as though
one were not as
much so from another
keep yours
crossing
the treat putting
a bun in the
oven tanker
up

learning not to
wait any more
than endless
teachers leaders law-
yers having a hard
day on't? multi-
national
chain substitutes

are still becoming
translate their product
economies to
reach you out
back blowback
reaching the droplets you're
sundered by
there's a mask
between you and
every tangible growth

you've got
left-overs
on your hands
from petting the car
again close-ish
near the air door
vault the truly
productive finish line
an endless
asphalt stage
sculpted through the
breathers
lucky road

For you're not
dead
exactly
close to home
its walls and windows
respiratory
to breeze

a subcon-
trastic change
filiates barbells
make your arms
of co-captivity
duress
you dress
the part of civic
gendarme inhaled
'I told you so'
in slabs on the front
lawn or firebell
muffled in the
basement dance
each cat arresting its
arithmetic
slumber
walks the walk

pat down
the rules of every
mouthful
near the bed leaves
trees huffed
there to

hide the history
anyone still
swigging the gift
of Finitude got very Near
which makes you
feel

plug-ins and
fine app arts co-
extend
their mercantiles of
blandishment
pretty pretty so-so
turn your
self out near

piled-up articles of coast
line the pockets of
a life vent stuck
your arms out

lower
legs to find
you're camping in
some other idea
of the generous what
magnitude of shake
nor tasty real
serves up
your back deck
breakfast lunch and
snack-time adds your
right to pay
conviction
clambers in
the chamber
of a purple
one whole year

you find a strong
cup helpful
to brush teeth with
you can hold
its blank
surrender
often
fractions of an outside
turn your chorus
art to
stands on grid

though any guilt
from not dying
stays so over
itself you're the one
dangling DNA
across the dream
shot from a dislocate
and absent
arms

in the yard are
Replace-
ment strategies
one box for an
other Full
of harm magnets
you can tweak and fling
them toward a
catchment
cull of stuff
resembling
vita oh
the yard is full
of ghosts
so animals and eatables
all the fruit and
misdirection
flanks dry hills
credibly turned

up from a prior
oceanic press-
ure totally
not here

Tell yourself stories of
perfection rot
fine documents
circa land
pools every
where transnational
circa newly won
bought chemicals
new fissures
in the antique documents
pouring in
between the cities
circa where the lumber
goes the slum plots
where you
not to ask for
bread

so tellingly
multiple dictions we're
sorry what
could we possibly
miss? no
rankling in the
diatribe of Economy
whose mouth sucks
on the buber I and thou
look hotly to contest
rank Meaning
fibs the statisticians
trying really hard
to hold
their arms up
to the heads
of anyone
listen

to turn a corner
dime store host
everyone
pops out from
their infamy
game on question
in fine form teleprompt
'I'm ok today'
as thought flies
close to the strata
of the advertised

you're well
again you're
well enough to
leave a load of
exhumate
paced in a muddy
growing floor
where someone's
gross percent
peaks out so
forced to pay intention
from the cabinet
where a power suck
cleans their death

so really very
absent of wet
so turned
a corner a
vacuum of
weight selves
newly
banged on walls

you turn on
the light and
become
official discourse

raw principality
markers
wedged inside
conducive
barriers
where they teem
and writhe
the zones astride
the light
are also
sourced
they ride the ambi-
valent principalities
straight in-
to the bark
partway
at least

covering your
living place with
felt
you
reveal large
operations
screenage
like the show
you are
watch this
hic talk

revel
wait again

the matting's
very
convince
one thick damp thread
cone-struck
in the unconceal
like everything
around here
is a re-fit
WW2
the batting
the prerogatives
elbow maps
ideas of what's
sheer

you very strong-
ly consider
reinhabiting the
token
there's a tablecloth
every nice
beside the planet

song comes up
pica pica
synchronic
babble
a recreation of
what the light
turns on
dinner's ready
again

3

Green tickets
fly around
gifty falling
sideways
from the telly
a mess-
age for your mouth
less
content-tape

you run with
tongue-hold
in the
room-weight
up with
libel's
equanimity
for why not
all the data's
informational
it's To Choose

lying close to you
the sheets
a rest

one by one
the filaments
cement or
make that
i.e. cursive
your blood
bound temper
electrifies
where plants
would like-
ly grow no
reason

environmental back
ground hosts
scry
quite close to the real
material
depending from
more furniture
one takes a
board wipe be-
come

toxic blastoids
screwed up
a courage
similar to washing
fruits and vegetables
with you
in the bath

tromp weights rolling
bubbles galore
you test them in
a mouth soap
tastes so good
such 'natural' predictions
us for animal

folly vents
tiny quasi animate
with an undeniable miss-
ion style
derange their
sleeves carefully
inside the box

Out from under or
over this
preen fest
stocky smudge
self-casing
to find the spot
one is
in like paradigm
like cream candies
seethe
emaciation

there's a new
die cast
model
replicant techno
wield
a selfhood seen
very over
screened
that's what
online shelving
maybe makes
a bracket
though
it might be noted
sucking
offer candy's
like the jukebox
playing when

someone else has paid
a song you like or
grew accustomed
to hear
when down time were
acutely
soft

such graft
it's always you
assert
& it rolls over
feedbank
splurged out
rosewater
on the bench
rezone
the small plate
full of
one

Whose onramp
chair now
seats you
saltimbanque

here's your offertory
peaked in-
efficient
no trouble

judgy screeds
pair their temper
with thermo-
nucleotides
you wait
until the chair is
true
with you

it's April
a day when
sometime in a future
dates
roll out
your tongue

if every life mats
equally
then what's on life?
green operants
bright birds but
elements

a voice plan gets
very near
one's open channels
call out Soybean
republic
Hampton replicants
such names

called once you're
naked at
bottom
no one to see
hub on planetary
spooning
world flick
eye looms
eating heads

your screens
simmer
wholly lapse
on selves
fuckumentary
if only

it's as
though
the belly
thighs
asshole &
genitals

kneecaps
straitened feet
twitchy calves
whole fields
somatic
sempiternity

knot out
the picture
carven
looper time
off screed
for grace or
popcorn we do
hunk
and roll

Arbor vitae
fern
hello
the mind's

like itself
amidst the parse
green as
footfalls
down the
hill

every time
how long
amidst the trees
go in
go out
tease mortality
pretty trees

fully administered
out of the belly
all invaginations
tiptoe
getting to
know
individually
crypt toe
thru the two lips
every trust
darker inside
haggis of warm core
emulates
how it's new life
topside
out

I drink
whose tea a
raffle
mug flicker
mats harl
broken on a head
conked road
up and down
legs im-
paired do
walk

a latent chord
strike
twitches oh
a stative
forest Pathogen
rise the
morning
quick fusions
in like Singapore
workers

cloister
tin-can careen

sweet money
how you darken
artificially
like suck
the moisture
out of salt
crystallize
whose be

lingual paradiso
splayed
over the room set
each sheet
barking
each head lamp
inside gutsy
tasseography
comes to pay
similitude
its planned
community
manqué

every touch
signifies an
accumulate for ghost
piled up
big accident on the ghost!
hassle hats
host tossers
pulling their share
truckily
carven out interior
space

you take
the stapler to
your laptop and
socket wench
obtuse
stapler on'ts fit!
rangier fingers
pick a separate
rote
ungaudy
psychedelia
hold non-
exist
edge
what will talk
and not
to each
other

the stapler makes
a hub
its black bat
commissive
fidelity cave
can be breathed

Come here austere
advances
clouds sticky up
bub
how we've hurt the
correspondent
window glass
making it all right
for you
oh king, fall of
facsimile
you think you
conch
myth

my feet are now
upside the top
the sea
to me's afloat
and all that
err
t'other side
hand me down
alveoli
oh lung
the smallest feet
crimped in
pushing oil
deep to
rub it in
glassy
walk inside
the water's
sharp and fined

gotholalia
's part of it
ink-mar
on the punt
page in hunt
gree
for you I
gree for
you

near here's
a buried lover
text whose arms
reach round
pink sunt

having kept it
at it
in the pocket
dense sur
e-world after arm-
ish she folds
up she's in
fold the
sheet

to-do the spun
body depend-
ing from the trunk
a bridge
span or between
strands
sand the
paper

could you see
andante
seize his
ambient virgule
a little rod
scratch
pick
on the other side
footpress
at the edge I mean
the water symbol
mark invert
staying in hole
wet feet
holding not up
out 'cause
that's directive
non a tribute
dicked up thru
a fissule on
which ramparts
hit their clay

here on the other
side of
Latin
talk to me
sweet miss

between the
palilalia
it's a bribe to keep
the embed
body count
up

4

We're catholic now
small c
purred dense with
staves
sudden on set
we're watch
our fingers
glued
each falling nurse
practitioner
doctor
so and so
splits names
inside us
body aura
one two four
match frieze

your sud fren
finds a fizz
turps it
openly flip
top we
can extend
out the bronchioles they
non align
their new
luffs
co detruit
inside the txt
we find an
other and she's
temper temper
endive
bitter intybus
an earl in an open
part oncurled
welcome
in alike
marsupial
down there
we heard you
ear to ear
composite
lustening

tense sex
toys with you
wired orifice
blanch out
for no two fausts are
like
key rooms
repetition tech-
no what's decide
stuck per
evensong dense
filiates in good
by your
dreams offer
succour
absence with-
out nor hic
or win
small grievance
witches
gender
rules against
the wind burnt
oddment

take the feature pull
it out cross-
length don't reach
down
reach down
your fill station
pants nor not to
trench

the text is yours
press enter
to insert a lot of
babies will
appear
pant life has
multo causative
many mouthful
luckies look to
forward to
scurry part
skit out
it'll haunt them
seechly
handing love
lean hear it
break such
small art
luff a wind

it listens at the
dark beach
shou shoough
no absence
is there
birds are the wind's
ears
lash wholly
darkened buttes
aflank

The prise is
not to be
wit less
at the outfoot
or thot have been
left amidst
in-thought

a curl ball
ghostened
wish to nuncio
at the frontage
right at
cull

to urn my text
sunder all felt
coasters
under them
to kern
stile gentures
in wit terse
ogling the urban over-
bites on which
runners copy
and do tell
falling of the balconies
repeatingly

a totally translate
wire velos
cure my clef
mouth stuck
at the barer
all infold
capital billot
coring
raser
their limbs 're
gabble
lolls are
flanker
unlast bref

I mean to under
lease zip
ocean make a
shirt
go shirt go
burn out
cilice
nonesuch cant we
melodize every
which way
catch a breeze
make out to demon-
strate look how
look the fringe
is balsam it's a
turgid
hove
to sling by
wear it
alter piece redo
pull out
your lungs re-
do

there's a scrap
some one's
gutting the fleuve
if you put your
mouth through
will it shill

your visit
burtle intake
koru
crunch as
breath?

drill a hole and
the individual
death
dealt blows
residual tangi
monarchs flown
off stream
for day bots
each like
breathers
picked in earth
pant tailor
stitching out
the thread inside
your blood

a million sinces
spring
your inner body
brewed there
high as
sever
gathered your
thin forest you're
a plan on

a bicycle many
photo graphs
posted for
an in between
gut miles
sounds of walk
a waver

the sheet screen
night whale
breaks its
blow by
blow
convincible
breech

it brings the air
up from on sea
maieutic
onset
flame
apocraphy

that surface wears
an option
flick
right from the
heart-
wood table
near to
one can
breath

under a press
the ink juts
fare on course
like blood on
blood
this day can
leak its
whalish parts
a petri dish
our entry
lidded cull
from out a lower
whale-cloud's
tannin
bet?

so reach kept
many optal
shin
dig fingers
who
we fretted
video pockets
more for more

hull an otherness
biddable fledge
to turn out
implements
dredge the
morning broke its
temperature
a gull
awoke and
turned its bed
outdoors the
newspaper
is
definite
apparently

hull's frictionless
to be found
thru turns on
turn
a bait
meant cut parts
where you put
yourself for
breakfast
there's a rivet in
the sky
it's not going
anywhere
soon

even if the news
turns
it won't alter
cast
the light hereby
you see? so
infamy patrols
its variance
keeps coming
the facts are
spread so fully
nothing doing
you can't
vestibule
oracular

so I'm digging in
the actual
equivalence machine
it digs
where news
lands so
incessant cracks
they call

echoes of a knock
death's busy
it's nice to be able
to ask
friends over
though we interface
on those lean
felts arguably
somebody's there
ready
to change
your channels
set worldometers
to feed
themselves
if only

5

Numbers flutter
leafs again a
thousand
birds breathe
haumanu
soon
part them-
selves inside
the airplane's
wing

how many
brackets
crown
your breath in-
tangible
hill side walks
a tremble
flash feet
bid or architect
unmasked

the globe's a
round thing with
fuzzy coordinates
proliferating
it's a mirror
look look the
ambulatory
memes
crawl on your skin
each story
draws the
attributes of
lent
around the next
box your attempts

you open
two eyes spoon
bowls inside
your headmouth
every hole turns
page blank
tributes
hone on pull
the scrip the
blow-through
hull

whose pheno-
scope
arrears
on flags
a Code does
all the buildings
raw
tweaked pharmacy
flut
side walk
flesh in a trance
the shred fabric
closed
the hungry
methadone child
all pre
trans
figured
numb in the arms
chalk wield head
harder
outlines

to be too
true
come back
light shift
sun shards shred
continuity
laugh for

cause
the curled body
lumped on the major
bed
windows
already splint
with elemental
efficacy
permission from
what's outside
ways in
the house's tipped
an allocate
body calling
names continue

on the
floor ground
all the mystery's
won out of
life
the like gritty
congealed
micro-furniture
swabs
one's skin
giving a
hint of
glassy
futurity

you often
hear that
slime
is lovely
that it
consummates
noses snails
throats
the quick clear
cream of the
blister
so that's
futurity for you
rolling on the sidewalk
again

the streets full of
symbolic
deer paths
trodden
cheerful as money
one frame
one foot
ghosts the next
your attic lung
slime treats
breathing
like the

amphibrach
it's truly
impatient to
continue

Even underneath
your skein face
doctor, nurse
we salute you
without being
anywhere
near the border

the grief
lockdown and
groceries
are not
the same
yet
salt applies
to your face
anything
foraging
that room in
the compound-

complex
sentence
mar bait
roll around

outside
periwinkle
asinine
sky thoughts

lawn at-
tributes atop
tall buildings
skip
heart
like the green
moniker
strives

thump thump
the earth
bump's
preggers with gif
piling near that
top

but ho hold
keep the rooftop
buggers
cossey the fold
fair green
purpose
names ar-
riving

the pharm door
co-sack vents
throat men
openers
settle in yawns
the lungs crack
anonyms
without thought a
part

feral wheels
trip up
dog's mercury
distal
brew lands
spot-on in
soluble

leaks
into comestibles
hats
pathways
upend then

scurry homes
all the blues are
after yous
polite, see?
holding for your
friend
ships
sailing your numbs
away

just as
hauntology
declares its
verisimilitude
a tin can
beats the
officer
well a proxy
soldat
kind of
blank-yawn
civic order
soldering on
alarmly close

youth-
pipes
auction call
if all the
gunk came out
at once
there's
nothing at last
arrived!
a tempt-
ing co-
relation
atmosphere
the genitalia
gleam
on earth

the organs
want their own
mouths
inverted comas
exhumate
getting ready
forge
plonk
spat along
a floor
outlet of
manumission's
hunker state

omit all
anthromality
throw us
a map
a rope
a heavy can
do

my friend
writes
wit and
care words
I discover
electric
ink can
think
neither waste
nor gather
only
emergents
exeunt-
ing from
outside
in to
one another
case, hull

ACKNOWLEDGEMENTS

With thanks to Murray Edmond, John Hall, and Lila Matsumoto for first readings, to Nathan Hamilton and Boiler House Press for taking on the book as its publisher, to *Blackmail Press* for printing two pages as a poem, to Amaranth Borsuk and Lily Robert-Foley for their supporting words, to Duriel Harris and Laura Mullen for all the being there, and to Mark and Rowan for sharing love and creative action in our pandemic lockdown house.

Breach
By Lisa Samuels

First published in this edition by Boiler House Press, 2021
Part of UEA Publishing Project
All rights reserved
© Lisa Samuels, 2021

The right of Lisa Samuels to be identified as the author of this
work has been asserted in accordance with the Copyright, Design
& Patents Act, 1988.

Design and typesetting by Emily Benton Book Design
emilybentonbookdesigner.co.uk

Typeset in Arnhem
Printed by Imprint Digital, UK
Distributed by NBN International

This book is sold subject to the condition that it shall not, by way
of trade or otherwise, be lent, resold, hired out, stored in a retrieval
system, or otherwise circulated without the publisher's prior
consent in any form of binding or cover other than that in which it is
published and without a similar condition including this condition
being imposed on the subsequent purchaser.

ISBN 978-1-913861-32-2